Hi my name's Tractor Ted. Today we are going to see some big machines at work.

The farmer is building a new barn to store his grain in. The huge excavator is making the road to it.

It fills the articulated hauler.

TED 1

The articulated hauler can drive on very steep slopes.

It is big and fast.

Inside the barn the machines are hard at work.

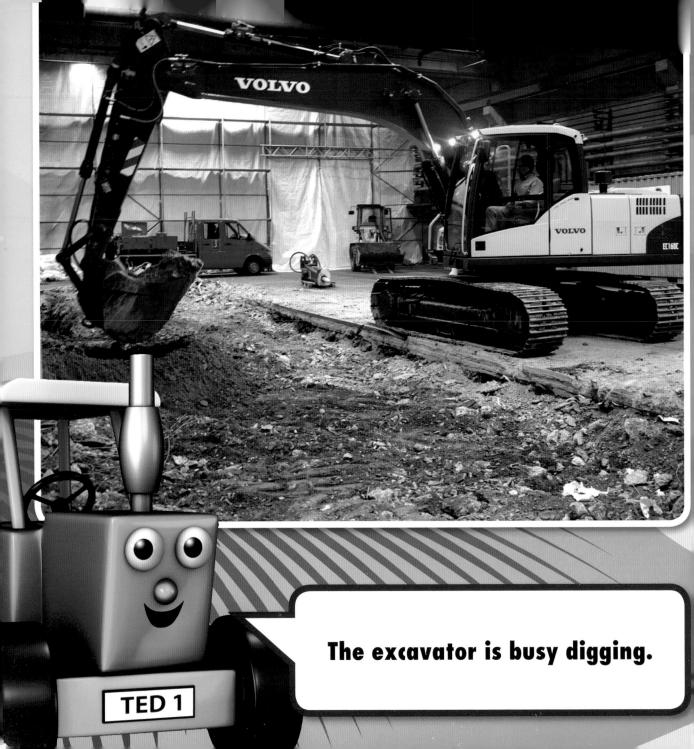

The excavator is busy digging.

TED 1

A concrete lorry pours cement onto the ground to make the floor.

What is the telehandler doing?

TED 1

It is putting the panels into place which will make the walls.

TED 1

Out in the field a huge combine is cutting the wheat.

Look at how big the header is.

As the combine cuts the wheat a tractor collects and bales the straw.

TED 1

The baler is very big and makes big bales.

The combine empties the grain into the trailer.

TED 1

It is nearly full.

There are two more tractors waiting. They will soon have their trailers filled.

TED 1

Here comes the tractor with the cultivator.

TED 1

The cultivator breaks up the ground after the wheat has been harvested.

Look - the tractor has caterpillar tracks instead of wheels.

CASE**IH**
QUADTRAC
535

This tractor has two sets of caterpillar tracks...

TED 1

...and this tractor has got huge wheels.
They will all stop the tractors getting stuck in the mud.

TED 1

The barn still isn't ready so the tractor has to tip the grain onto the ground.

Here is a digger. It has a backhoe on the back...

...and a bucket on the front.

TED 1

At last the barn is finished and the grain can be stored inside. What a good job.

After the long days work the farmer gives the combine a good wash.

TED 1

Was it the articulated hauler

Or the big tractor

Or the combine?

Which was your favourite big machine?

TED 1

Can you remember what this machine is called?

How many wheels can you count?